AWESOME Christmas
ACTIVITIES AND PAPERCRAFTS FOR KIDS

PUZZLES, GAMES, COLORING, GREETING CARDS, PAPER ORNAMENTS, RECIPES, AND MORE!

SKY PONY PRESS

Library of Congress Cataloging-in-Publication Data is available on file.

Illustrations credit: Shutterstock.com

Translation by Grace McQuillan

ISBN: 978-1-5107-5906-0

Printed in China

THIS ACTIVITY BOOK BELONGS TO:

_____

MEMORY GAME

1

Cut out the cards.

2

Mix them up and arrange them in rows.

3

Each player turns over two cards, one blue and one yellow. If the two cards match, place them down in front of you and play again. If you turn over two cards that do not match, turn them back over. Memorize where each card is located. Now it's the next player's turn to flip over two cards and try to find a match.

4

The player with the most matches wins!

MEMORY	MEMORY	MEMORY
MEMORY	MEMORY	MEMORY
MEMORY	MEMORY	MEMORY
MEMORY	MEMORY	MEMORY

MEMORY game

MEMORY   MEMORY   MEMORY

MEMORY   MEMORY   MEMORY

MEMORY   MEMORY   MEMORY

MEMORY   MEMORY   MEMORY

MEMORY	MEMORY	MEMORY
MEMORY	MEMORY	MEMORY
MEMORY	MEMORY	MEMORY
MEMORY	MEMORY	MEMORY

MEMORY GAME

7

MEMORY MEMORY MEMORY

MEMORY MEMORY MEMORY

MEMORY MEMORY MEMORY

MEMORY MEMORY MEMORY

9

PUZZLE GaMe

CUTOUTS

1

To make the puzzle pieces more rigid, glue them to pieces of cardstock before cutting them out. Use cardstock in different colors so you can tell the three puzzles apart. Cut out the puzzle pieces along the dotted lines.

2

Shuffle the pieces and put the puzzle back together.

3

Time yourself to see if you can finish the puzzle faster and faster!

PUZZLE

11

PUZZLE

PUZZLE

CHRISTMAS
ORNAMENTS

1

Cut out the ornaments and color them in.

2

Use a hole puncher to make a hole
in the top of the ornament.

3

Thread a piece of string or pretty ribbon through
the hole and tie a knot. Hang the ornaments on
your tree or on a ribbon to make a garland.

PIXELS

Use the color code to color each box,
and at the end you'll have a beautiful picture!

SPIRAL garland

CUTOUTS

1

Color the spiral.

2

Cut out the spiral along the dotted lines.

3

Use a hole puncher to poke a hole in the center and attach a ribbon.

4

Unfold the spiral garland like an accordion and hang it on your tree.

24

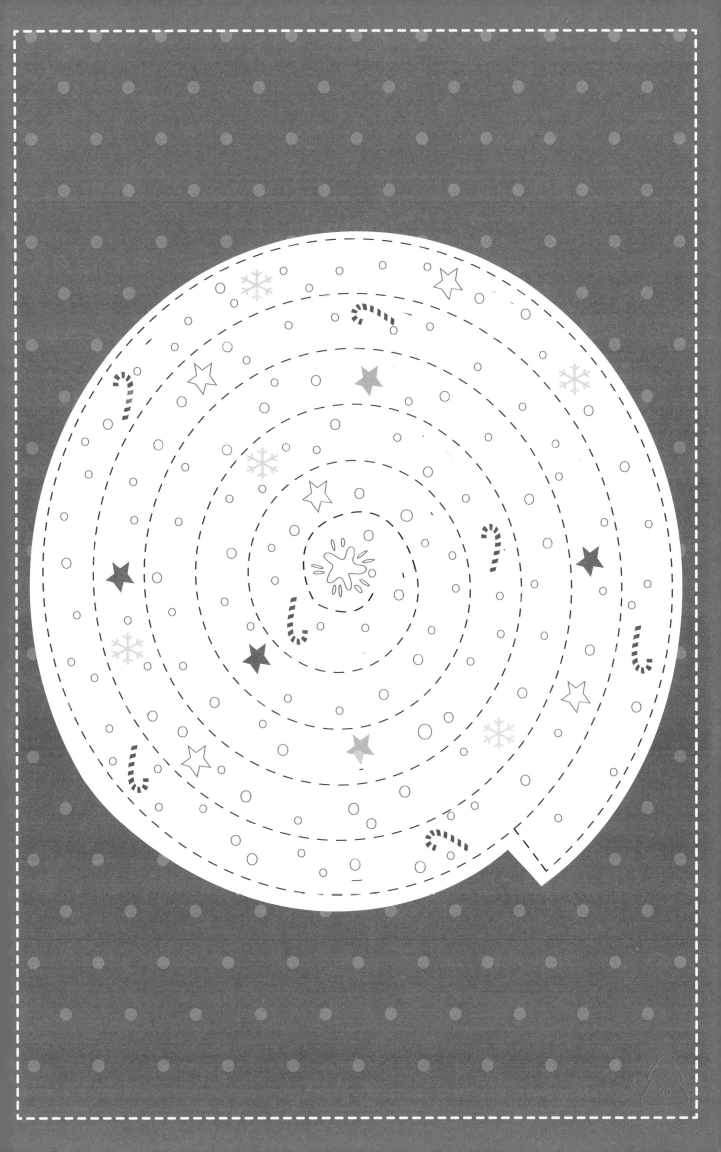

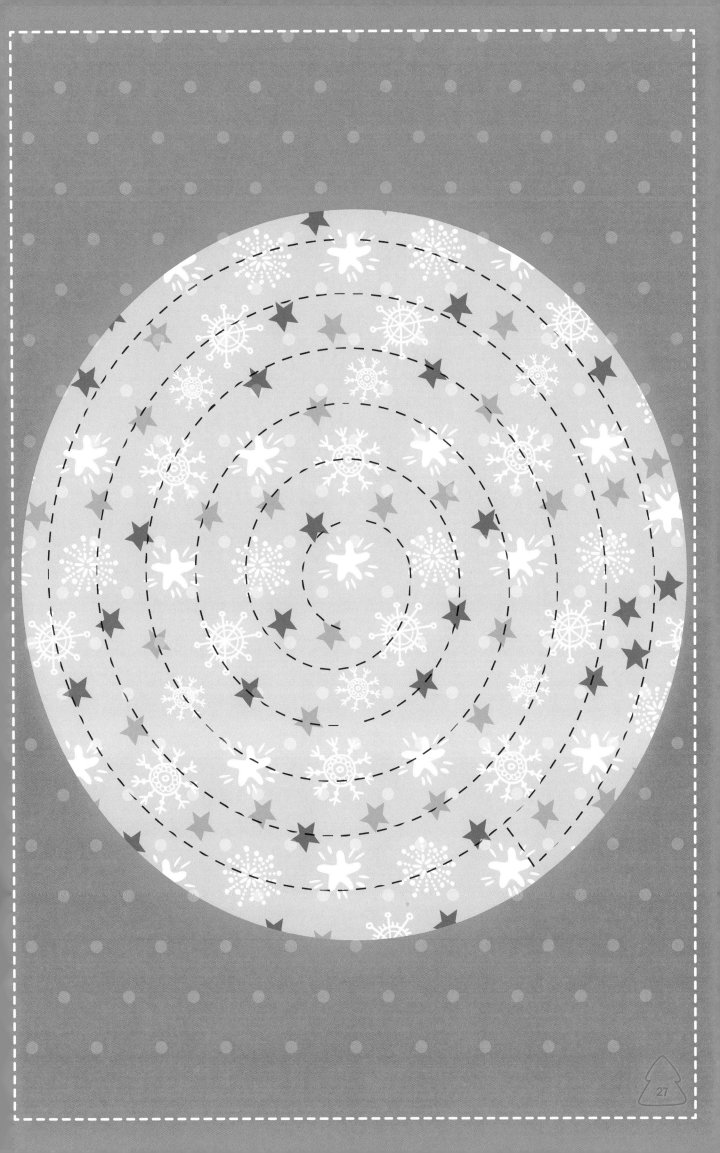

28

MAZE
Help the penguin find his hat.

29

PENNANT
Banner

1

Cut out the pennants.

2

Fold the pennants in half.

3

Put a little glue on the inside of each pennant then attach them to a ribbon or pretty string to make a superb Christmas banner.

31

32

34

MATCHING

Draw a line from each character
to their missing item.

CHRISTMAS SNOWFLAKES

CUTOUTS

1

Cut out the circle.

2

Fold the circle in half along the dotted lines, then in half again, then in half again so the drawing is on the outside.
For the snowflakes on pages 39 and 41, you will have to fold one more time.

3

Cut along the dotted lines, then carefully unfold the snowflake.

4

Color your snowflake, then hang it on a piece of clear string or attach it to your window.

40

41

42

SANTA'S WORKSHOP

1

Cut out the figurines on the following pages along the dotted lines (you can glue them to a piece of cardstock before cutting them out to make them more rigid).

2

Fold the bottom to make a base.

3

Use a cardboard box (an old shoebox would work) to make Santa's workshop. Cut out a door and windows, then decorate it with colored pencils.

4

Use the figurines to bring Santa's workshop to life.

46

48

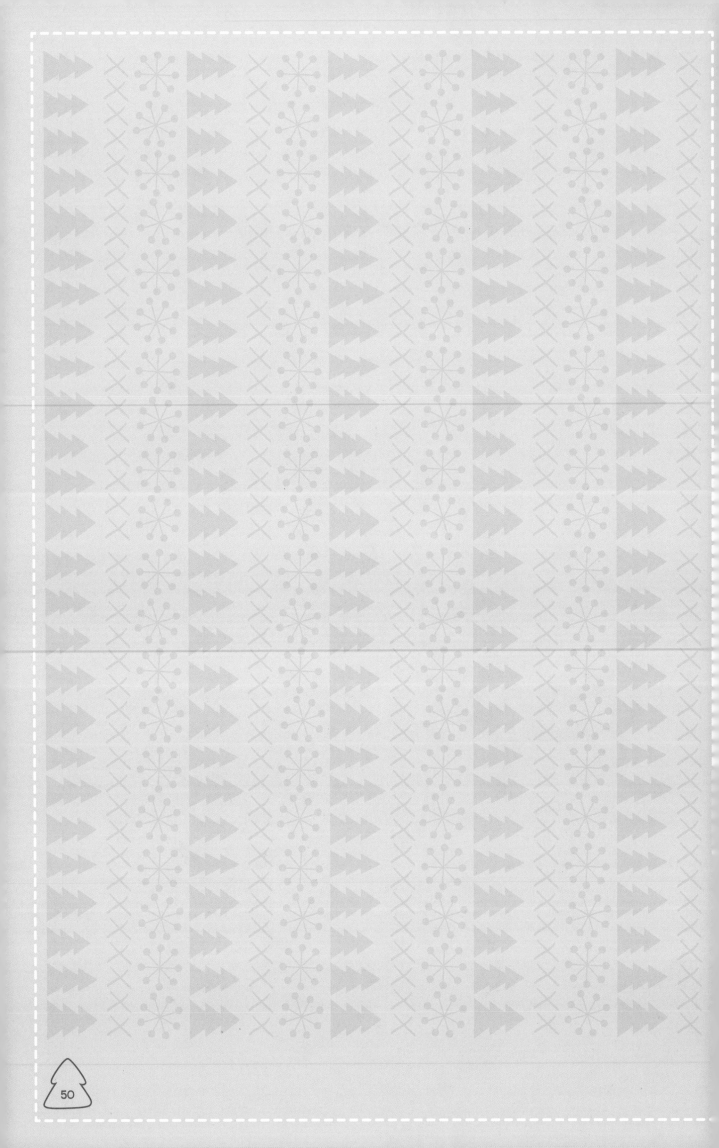

50

SPOT THE
DIFFERENCES
Find the 6 differences
between the two pictures.

CHRISTMAS
PUPPETS

Cut out all of the parts of the puppet.

Use a hole puncher to poke holes.

Attach the parts of the puppet
together with brass fasteners.

Glue the hat onto the head,
then glue a photo of yourself
onto the puppet's face.

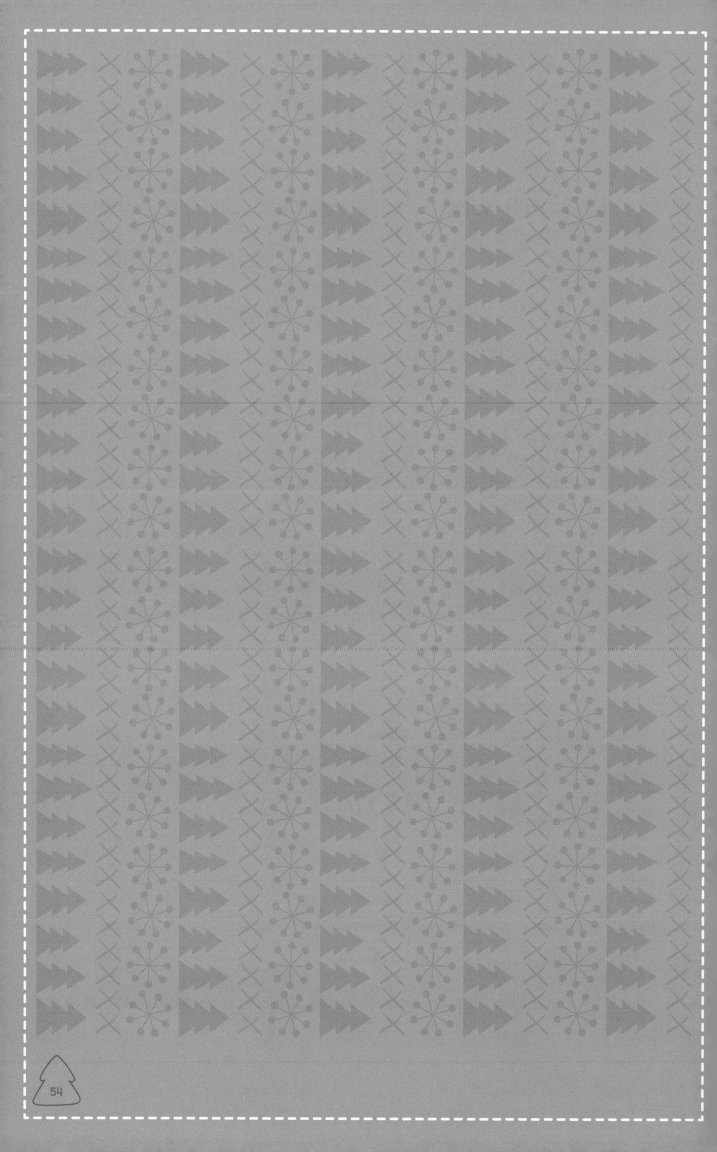

54

Glue the beard and hat onto Santa Claus's head, then draw eyes and a nose.

55

Glue the scarf and hat onto the snowman's head, then glue on the nose.

58

Glue the scarf and antlers onto the reindeer's head.

60

SUDOKU

Fill in all of the empty boxes so that:
• Each row contains the numbers 1 through 4.
• Each column contains the numbers 1 through 4.
• Each square 2 x 2 box contains the numbers 1 through 4.

3			2
	4		
	2	1	
1			2

SANTA CLAUS
paper craft

1

Cut out the pieces along the dotted lines.

2

Glue the hat ❶ onto the head ❷. Glue on the hat brim ❸ to hide where the other pieces are attached.

3

Glue the mustache pieces ❹ and ❺ to the bottom of the head.

4

Glue on the bowtie ❻, and then glue the knot ❼ in the middle of the bow.

5

Fold the top of the hat forward and glue on the pompom ❽.
Draw two eyes and you will see Santa Claus's face.

LOGIC

Which picture should you put in the circle so that
each object appears once in every row and every column?

Choose the correct answer.

1

2

3

HAPPY
HOLIDAYS

1

Cut out the greeting cards.

2

Color the inside and write a nice message for someone you love.

3

Give out your cards or put them in envelopes to send in the mail.

GREETING CARDS

HAPPY NEW YEAR

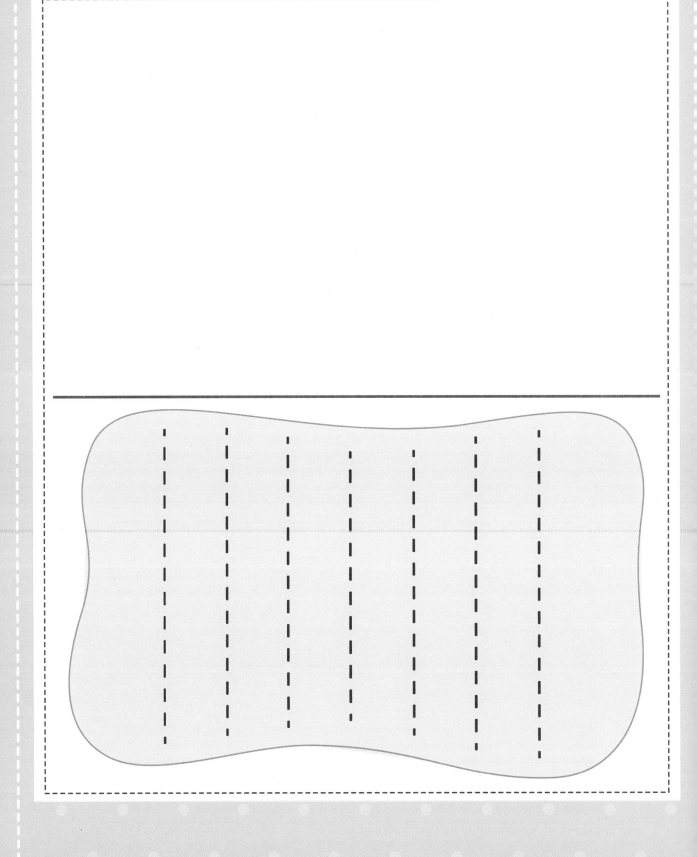

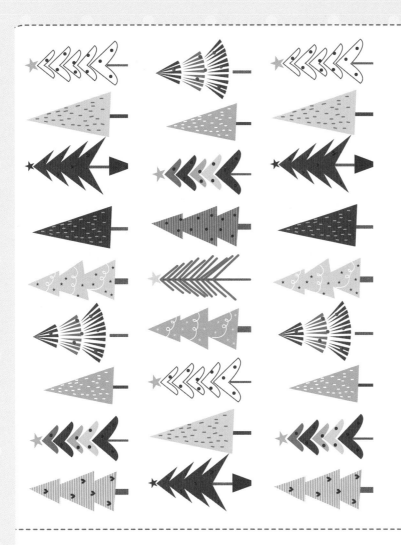

MERRY CHRISTMAS

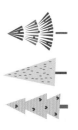

69

MERRY CHRISTMAS

WHERE IS MY
CHRISTMAS TREE?

One of these Christmas trees is missing
its matching partner. Find which one it is.

73

POP-UP card

Fold the sheet in half.

Cut along the solid lines and
fold along the dotted lines.

 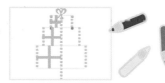

Color and decorate the presents!

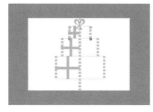

Put glue on the back of your decorated sheet and
glue it inside the space indicated on page 77.

76

Glue your card here.

MAZE

Help the rabbit choose the right path to find his little sister.

MY FOLDING
Christmas Tree

Cut out the shapes on the next page and fold them as shown in the steps below. You will then have two beautiful Christmas trees to glue on a card. Decorate the trees with lights and pretty ornaments.

1

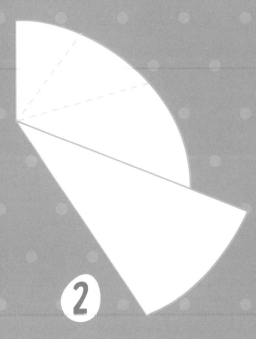

2

3

4

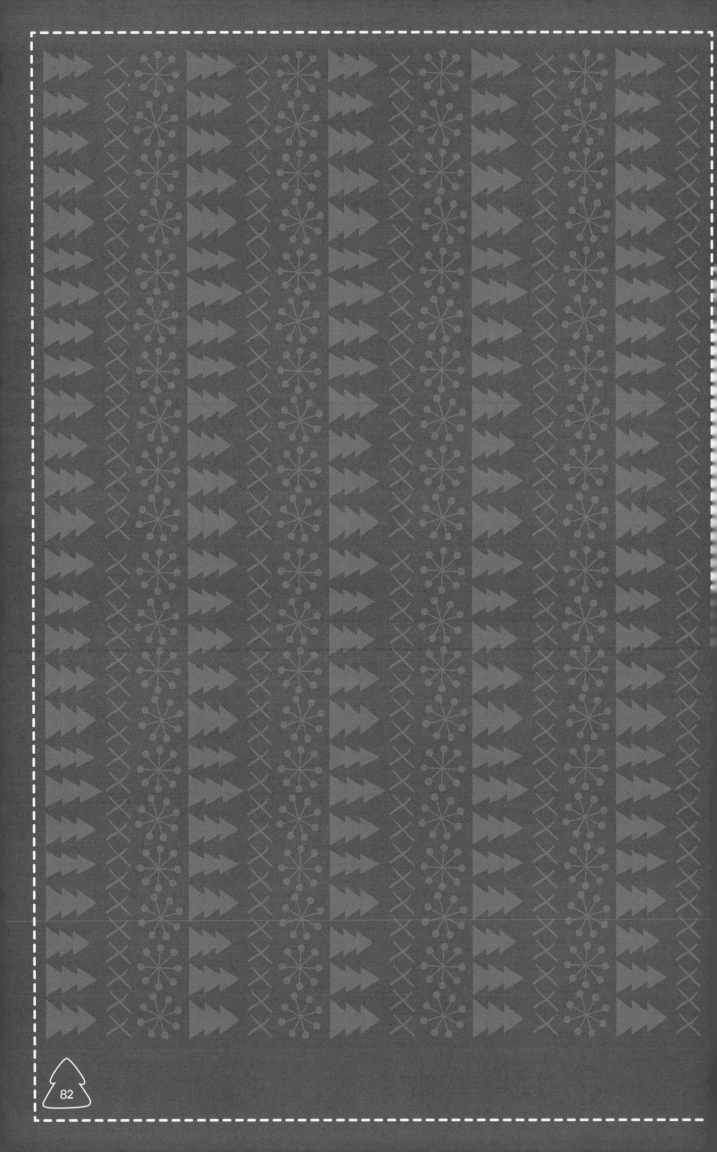

MY CHRISTMAS
tree craft

Cut out the pieces of the Christmas tree,
then glue them onto a card.

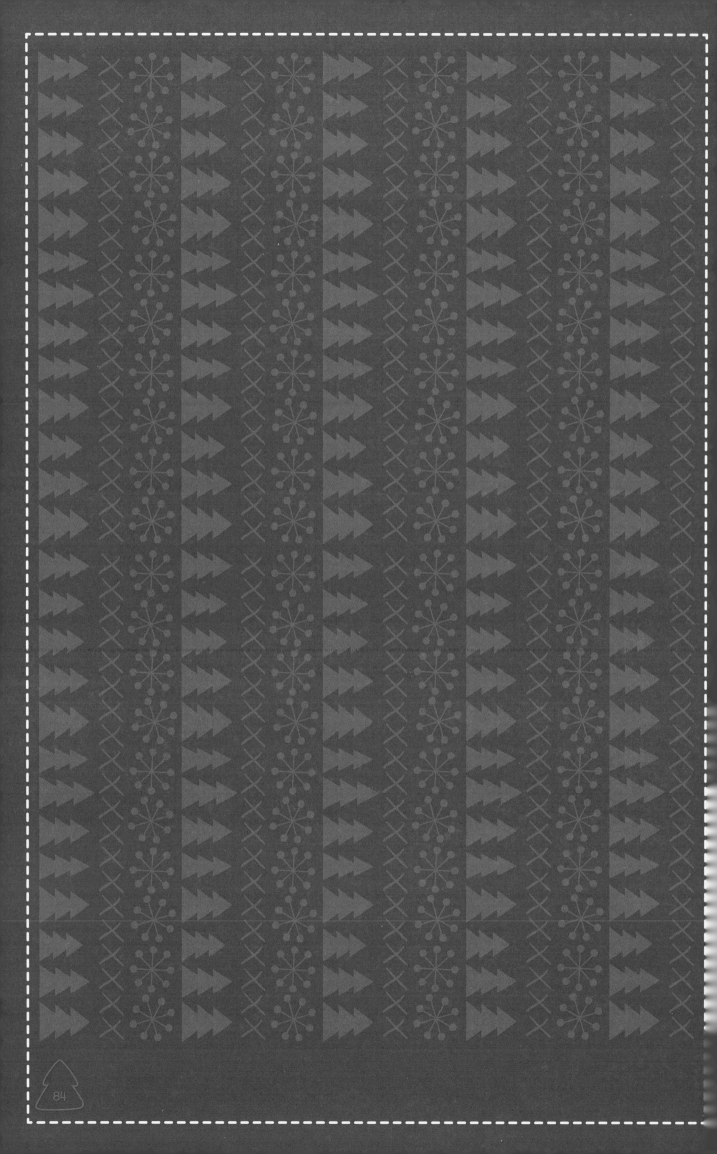

SUDOKU

Fill in all of the empty boxes so that:
• Each row contains the letters A, B, C, and D.
• Each column contains the letters A, B, C, and D.
• Each square 2 x 2 box contains the letters A, B, C, and D.

C			B
B	A		D
			C
			A

CHRISTMAS
GIFT TAGS

1

Cut out the tags.

2

Use a hole puncher to poke a
hole in the top of each tag.

3

Thread a piece of string or pretty ribbon
through the hole, tie a knot, and attach one
tag to each present.

MERRY
CHRISTMAS

HAPPY
NEW YEAR

HAPPY
HOLIDAYS

88

_____'s

room

PIXELS

Use the color code to color each box,
and at the end you'll have a beautiful picture!

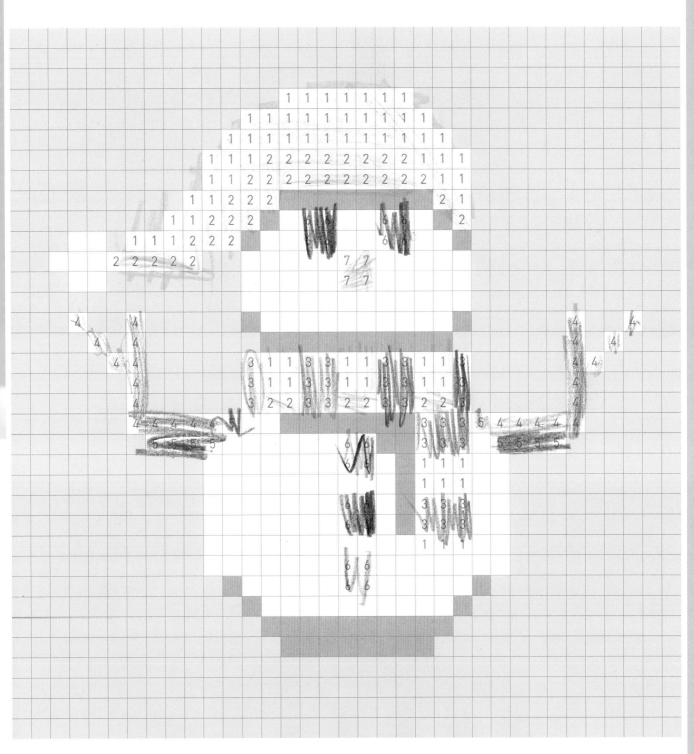

1 2 3 4 5 6 7

IDEA
BOX

1 Cut out the idea box.

2 Fold the box along the dotted lines.

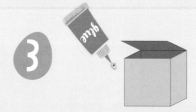

3 Put glue on flap 1, then glue the bottom of the box (the area also labeled 1).

Put glue on flap 2, then glue the side of the box.

4 Write your gift ideas on small pieces of paper and put them in your idea box.

GLUE HERE
Mets de la colle ici ②

MY BOX
OF IDEAS

GLUE HERE ①

93

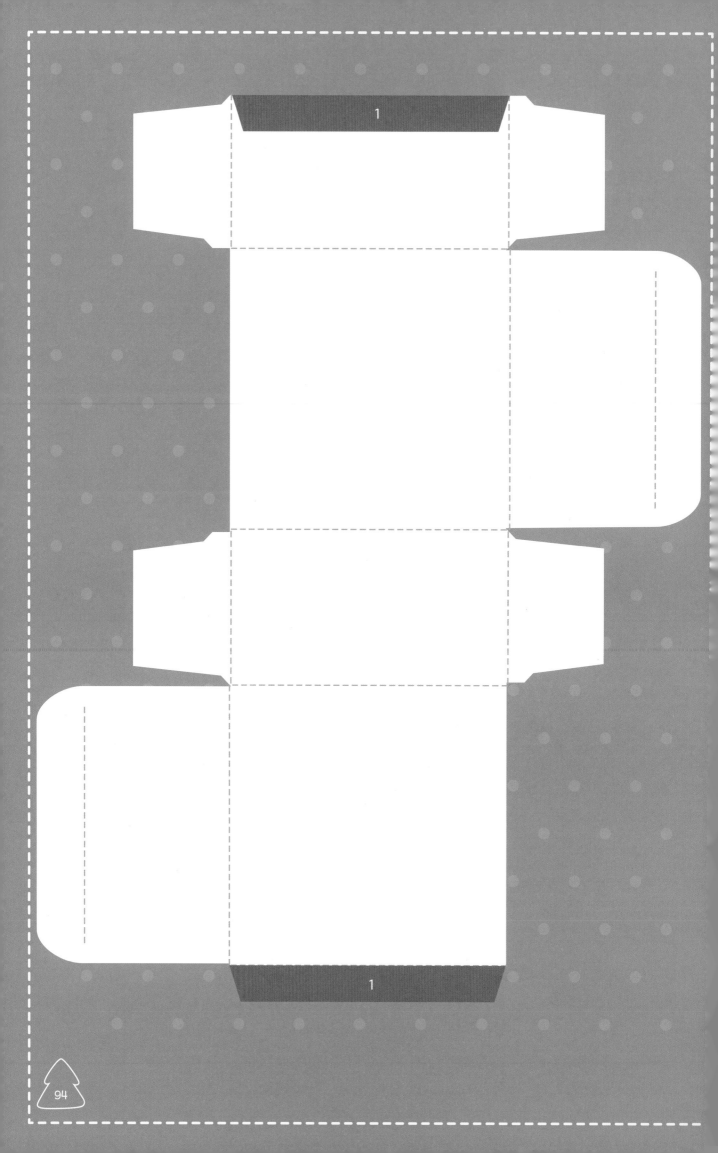

1

1

94

COUNT
THE ORNAMENTS
How many ornaments can you count?
Write your answers in the circles.

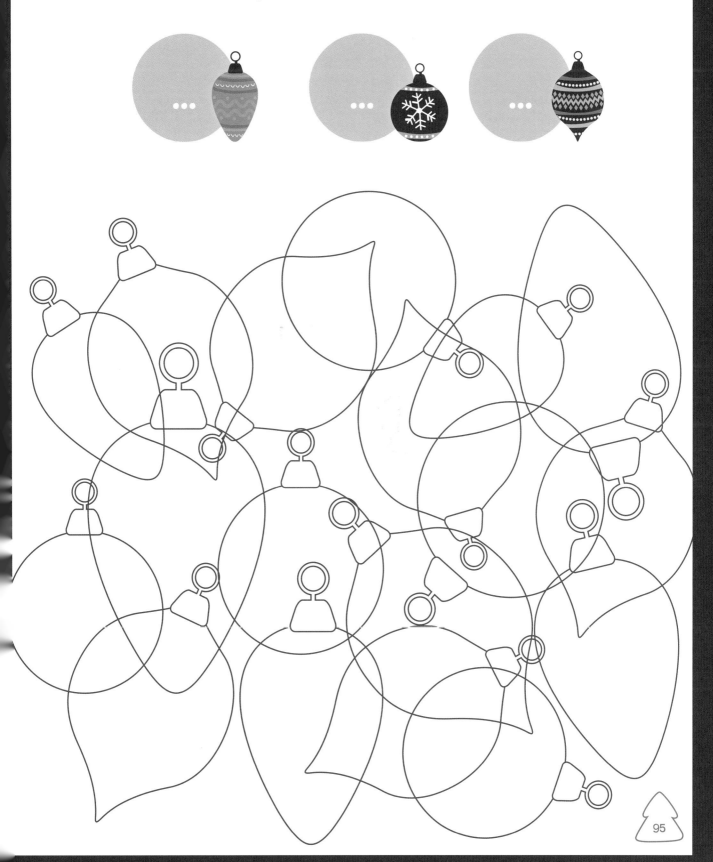

WRITING
TO SANTA CLAUS

1

Cut out the following pages to prepare your list of gift ideas and your letter to Santa Claus.

2

Write a nice message to Santa Claus.

3

SANTA CLAUS
1 SANTA CLAUS LANE
NORTH POLE

Put your letter in an envelope and mail it.

MY GIFT IDEAS

DEAR SANTA CLAUS

My name is _____

and I am _____ years old.

I live in _____

next to _____

Draw or glue on pictures of the presents you would like to get for Christmas.

This year I was

⭐ very good

⭐ pretty good

⭐ almost good

So, I would like you to bring me:

_____

_____

_____

_____

Thank you, Santa Claus!
I hope you have a Merry Christmas.
Lots of kisses to you and the elves and all of your friends at the North Pole.

I'd also like you to bring presents

for: _____ Signature: _____

SUDOKU

Color the rest of the stockings so that:
• Each row contains one stocking in every color.
• Each column contains one stocking in every color.

101

BINGO

CUTOUTS

1

Cut out the 4 playing boards and the 24 cards. To make them more rigid, you can glue them to a piece of cardstock before cutting them out.

2

Mix up the cards and place them face down on the table. Each player takes 1 playing board. (If there are 2 players, each one takes 2 boards.)

3

The first player takes a card. If the card matches an image on his board, he places it on his board and plays again. If not, he places the card back on the table and the next player takes a turn.

4

The first player to fill their board wins!

BINGO

BINGO

BINGO

BINGO

BINGO

BINGO

BINGO

BINGO   BINGO   BINGO

BINGO   BINGO   BINGO

BINGO   BINGO   BINGO

BINGO   BINGO   BINGO

108

BINGO

BINGO BINGO BINGO

BINGO BINGO BINGO

BINGO BINGO BINGO

BINGO BINGO BINGO

CONNECT
THE DOTS
Connect the dots in numerical order,
then color the picture.

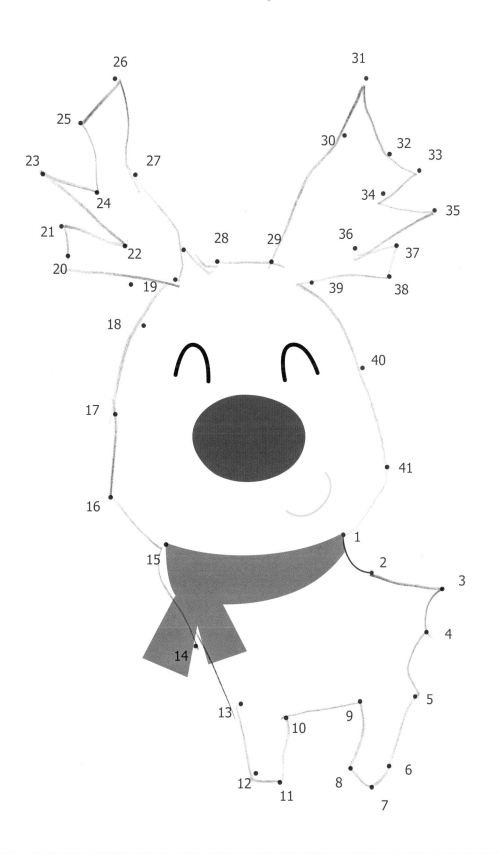

DOMINOES CUTOUTS

1
Cut out the 28 dominoes. To make them more rigid, you can glue them to a piece of cardstock before cutting them out.

2
Place the dominoes face down on a table. Each player takes 5 to 7 dominoes, depending on the number of players. The rest of the dominoes form the pile. The player who has the double Santa Claus places it on the table. If this double is in the pile, choose another double to start the game.

3
The next player places a domino with the same picture to the left or right. If he doesn't have one, he draws a domino from the pile. If the domino he draws matches the picture, he puts it on the table. If it does not, his turn is over.

4
The first player to put down all of his dominoes wins! If no one can play anymore, the player with the fewest dominoes wins!

DOMINOES

DOMINOES

DOMINOES

DOMINOES

DOMINOES

DOMINOES

DOMINOES

DOMINOES

DOMINOES

DOMINOES

DOMINOES

DOMINOES

DOMINOES

DOMINOES

DOMINOES

DOMINOES

DOMINOES

DOMINOES

116

DOMINOES

117

DOMINOES

DOMINOES

DOMINOES

DOMINOES

DOMINOES

DOMINOES

DOMINOES

DOMINOES

118

DOMINOES

DOMINOES

DOMINOES

DOMINOES

DOMINOES

DOMINOES

MATCHING

Match the characters with
their favorite foods.

DREAM catcher

DREAMS

1

Cut out the circle, feathers, and stars on the following pages.

2

Use a hole puncher to punch holes in the bottom of the circle and in the tops of the feathers and stars.

3

Thread the holes with a piece of string or a pretty ribbon, tie a knot, and hang your dream catcher above your bed.

DREAMS

123

126

ADDING UP

How many of these objects do you see?
Circle each one and write your answers in the bubbles.

Presents **16**

Christmas Ornaments **6**

CHRISTMAS CHATTERBOX

1

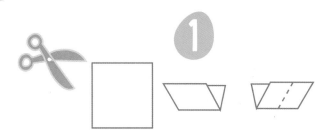

Cut out the chatterbox, then fold it in half in both directions to mark the folds in the center.

2

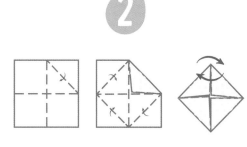

Fold the corners of the chatterbox toward the center, then turn the chatterbox over.

3

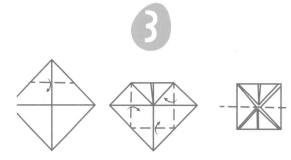

Fold the corners of the chatterbox toward the center again, then fold it in half.

4

Merry Christmas!

5

Pretend to be Santa Claus

3

Draw a picture of Santa Claus

Dance like Santa Claus

6

Name three presents you want this year

2

Sing "Rudolph the Red-Nosed Reindeer"

7

Pretend to be a reindeer

Draw a snowman

1

8

129

130

Create your own activities and write them on the triangles in the middle before folding your chatterbox.

132

PUZZLE

Look carefully and find a place for
each of the three missing pictures.

CHOCOLATE
YULE LOG

ASK AN ADULT TO HELP YOU MAKE THIS RECIPE.

YOU WILL NEED

5 eggs | 3 1/2 ounces (100 g) flour | 1 pinch of salt | 4 1/2 ounces (120 g) granulated sugar | Chocolate hazelnut spread or fruit jam

1 Separate the egg whites from the yolks. Add three quarters of an ounce (20 g) of sugar and the salt to the egg whites and beat them until they form stiff peaks.

5 eggs

1 pinch of salt

3/4 ounce (20 g) granulated sugar

2 Whisk the egg yolks together with three and one-half ounces (100 g) of sugar, then add the flour.

3 1/2 ounces (100 g) flour

Next, gently incorporate the beaten egg whites using a spatula.

3 1/2 ounces (100 g) granulated sugar

3 Pour the batter onto a baking tray lined with parchment paper. Bake for 12 minutes.

12 MINUTES IN THE OVEN AT **350°F**

4 Turn the cake out onto a damp dish towel and peel off the parchment paper. Roll the cake into a cylinder, leaving the dish towel on the inside so the cake does not dry out. Let cool completely.

5 Unroll the cake and cover with the chocolate hazelnut spread or fruit jam.

6 Roll up the cake again. Wrap in plastic wrap, making sure it is tight on both ends. Place the cake in the refrigerator for one hour to set.

CHRISTMAS
SHORTBREAD COOKIES

ASK AN ADULT TO HELP YOU MAKE THIS RECIPE.

(1) In a large bowl, mix together the brown sugar, flour, and salt until your dough looks like coarse yellow sand.

(2) Add the butter in small pieces and combine using the tips of your fingers.

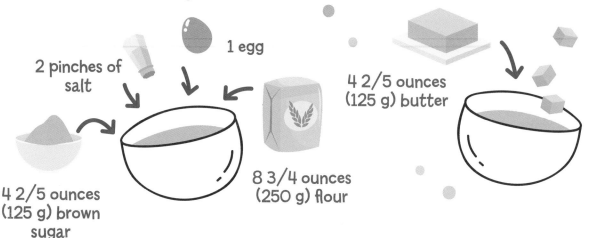

1 egg

2 pinches of salt

4 2/5 ounces (125 g) butter

8 3/4 ounces (250 g) flour

4 2/5 ounces (125 g) brown sugar

(3) On a floured work surface, roll out the dough to a thickness of 2 mm. Use a cookie cutter to cut out your shortbread cookies in the shape of gingerbread men. Place them on a baking tray and bake for 15 minutes.

15 MIN IN THE OVEN at 340°F

(4) In a bowl, mix together one-quarter of an egg white with powdered sugar until you have a smooth texture. Using a pastry bag or a paintbrush, decorate your gingerbread men.

1/4 egg white

Powdered sugar

136

CHOCOLATE
sausage

ASK AN ADULT TO HELP YOU MAKE THIS RECIPE.

1 Melt the chocolate and butter together using a double boiler method. Remove from heat and add the whole egg, whisking vigorously, then add the powdered sugar.

3 1/2 ounces (100 g) butter

3 1/2 ounces (100 g) powdered sugar

1 egg

7 ounces (200 g) baking chocolate

2 Crumble the cookies into small pieces and cut the marshmallows into quarters. In a large bowl, mix together the melted chocolate, cookies, and marshmallows.

10 marshmallows

melted chocolate

5 1/4 ounces (150 g) plain cookies

3 Pour the mixture onto a piece of plastic wrap. Fold the plastic around the chocolate to give it the shape of a big sausage. Refrigerate for six hours before slicing.

HIDE
and seek
The objects below are hidden in the drawing.
It's up to you to find them!

Mittens  Bird  Fox  Hedgehog

138

MAZE

Help Santa Claus find his sleigh,
then color the picture.

WHAT DOES
NOT BELONG?
There is a snowman hidden somewhere
on this page. Can you find it?

140

SUDOKU

Color the rest of the trees so that:
• Each row contains one tree in every color.
• Each column contains one tree in every color.

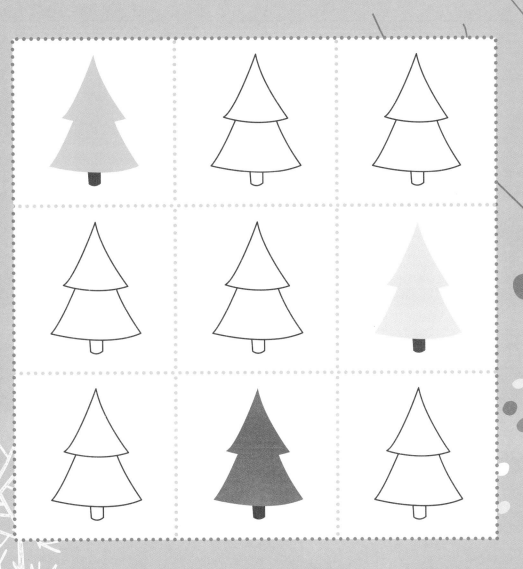

141

MATCHING
Pairs
These mittens have been mixed up.
Circle them with different colors to form pairs.

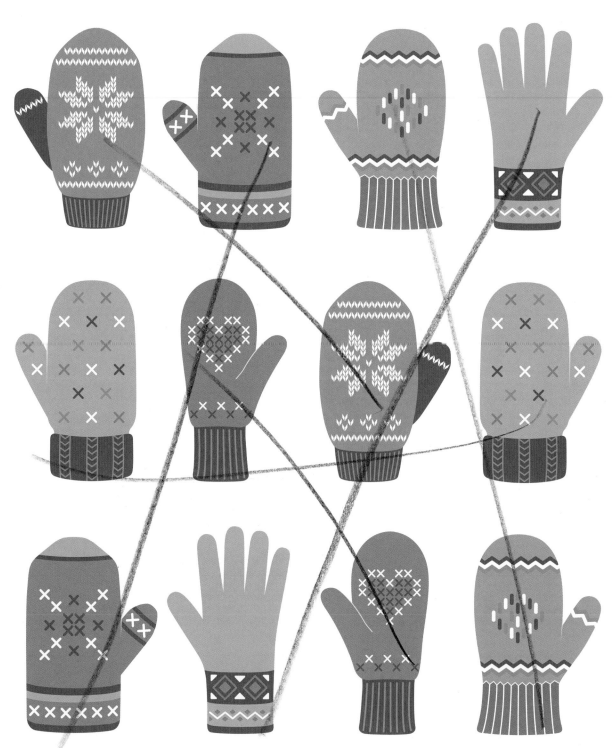

ADDING UP

How many foxes do you see?
Circle them and write your answer in the bubble.

WHERE IS
MY STOCKING
Can you find this stocking?

WHERE IS MY SHADOW?

Help the little girl find her shadow.

SUDOKU

Color the rest of the presents so that:
• Each row contains one present in every color.
• Each column contains one present in every color.

THE
RIGHT PATH

Help Santa Claus find the little reindeer.

DRAW A CHRISTMAS TREE

Use symmetry to learn how to draw a Christmas tree.
Decorate it with ornaments and color it in.

WHO DOES NOT BELONG?
Can you find this Santa Claus?

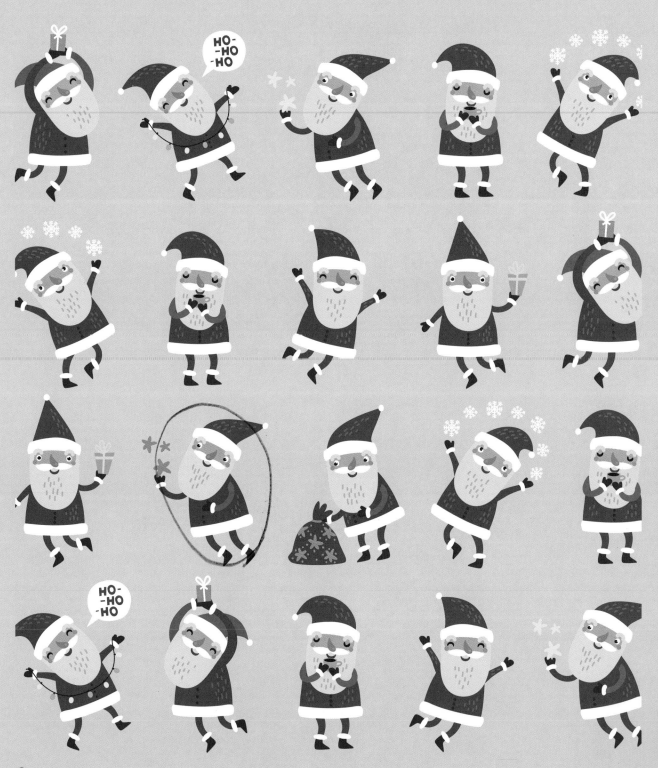

HIDE
and seek
Find these objects in the picture and circle them.

4   6   1

SPOT THE
DIFFERENCES

Find the 7 differences between these two pictures.

153

PUZZLE

Look carefully at the picture and
find where the missing picture pieces should go.

DRAWING

Trace over the dotted lines,
then color in the friendly owl.

155

CODED
MESSAGE

Use the code to find out where
Santa Claus's friends are meeting.

A E I O U

AT SANTA'S

WORKSHOP

SUDOKU

Color the rest of the stars so that:
• Each row contains one star in every color.
• Each column contains one star in every color.

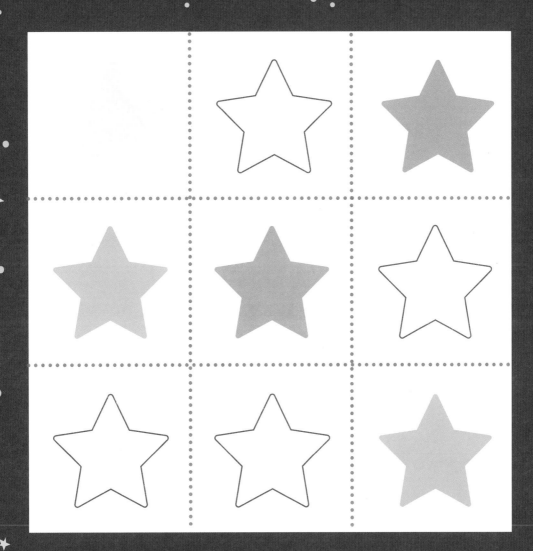

WHERE IS
MY SHADOW?

Draw a line from each character to its shadow.

SPOT THE
DIFFERENCES
Find the 5 differences between these two pictures.

PUZZLE

Look carefully at the image and
find where the missing picture pieces should go.

A   B   C

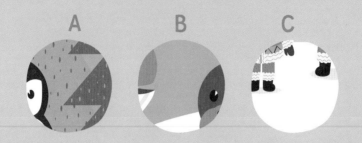

160

LOGIC

Which Christmas tree should go in the bubble
so that each kind of tree appears once in each row and column?

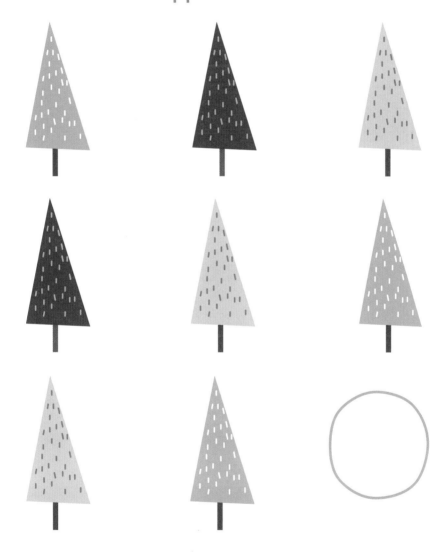

Choose the correct answer.

1   **2**   **3**

WHO DOES
NOT BELONG?

Someone here is disguised as a reindeer.
Do you see who it is?

163

CODED
MESSAGE

Use the code to find out
what is happening in Santa's workshop.

A E I O U

THE ELVES

ARE MAKING

TOYS

SUDOKU

Color the rest of the ornaments so that:
• Each row contains one ornament in every color.
• Each column contains one ornament in every color.

DRAW A
GINGERBREAD MAN
Use symmetry to learn how
to draw a gingerbread man.

PIXELS

Use the color code to color each box,
and at the end you'll have a beautiful picture!

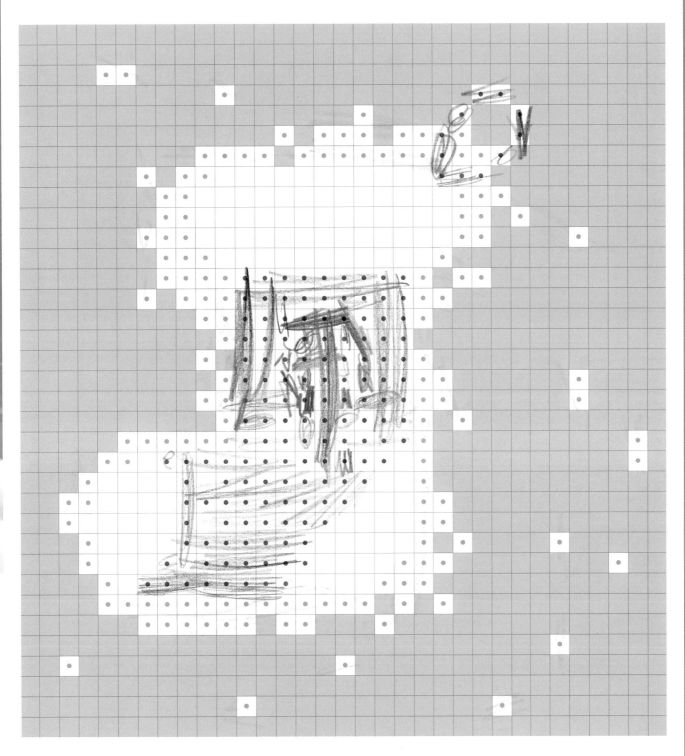

MAZE

Help the penguin find his friends,
then color in the snowflakes.

169

WORD
search

Find these words in the grid.
They can be written horizontally or vertically.

BEARD

SLED

HOLLY

```
S L E D H R B V
H N L T O V E P
O O F D L N A V
U E F S L M R Q
X L C Y Y Q D B
```

ELF

Stockings

Reindeer

ADDING UP

How many stockings and reindeer do you see?
Circle them and write your answers in the bubbles.

175

WHERE IS MY SHADOW?

Circle Santa Claus's Shadow!

DRAW
a present
Use symmetry to learn how to draw a present.

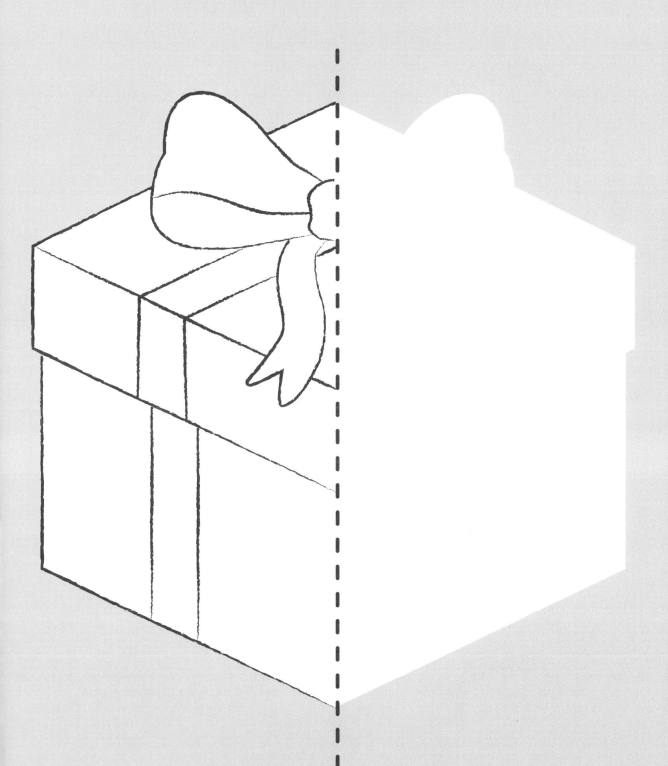

LOGIC

What should go in the bubble so that each
picture appears once in every row and column?

Choose the correct answer.

1   **2**   **3**

MATCHING

Draw a line from the bird, the polar bear,
and Santa Claus to the place where each of them lives.

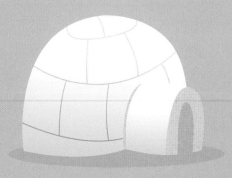

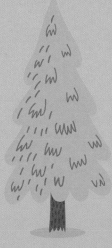

CODED MESSAGE

Use the code to find out what the little girl is saying.

A E I O U

I CAN'T WAIT TO OPEN MY PRESENTS

182

ADDING UP

How many winter hats with a pompom do you see?
Write your answer in the bubble.

185

THE RIGHT PATH

Find the path to help Santa Claus get back to his sleigh.

LOGIC

Which snowflake could we put in the bubble
so that each kind appears once in every row and column?

Choose the correct answer.

1   2   3

PIXELS

Use the color code to color each box, and
at the end you'll have a beautiful picture!

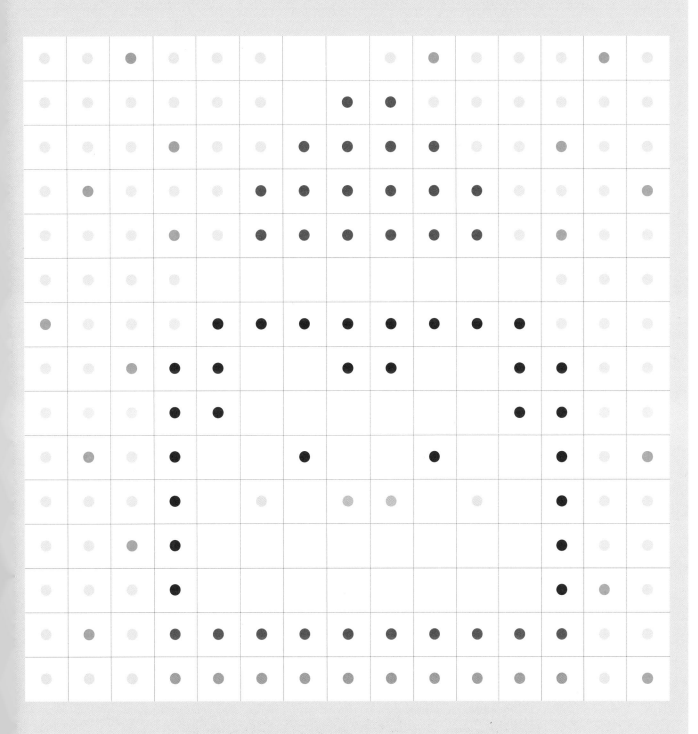

THE
RIGHT PATH
Help Santa Claus find
the path to the chimney.

SUDOKU

Color the rest of the stockings so that:
• Each row contains one stocking in every color.
• Each column contains one stocking in every color.

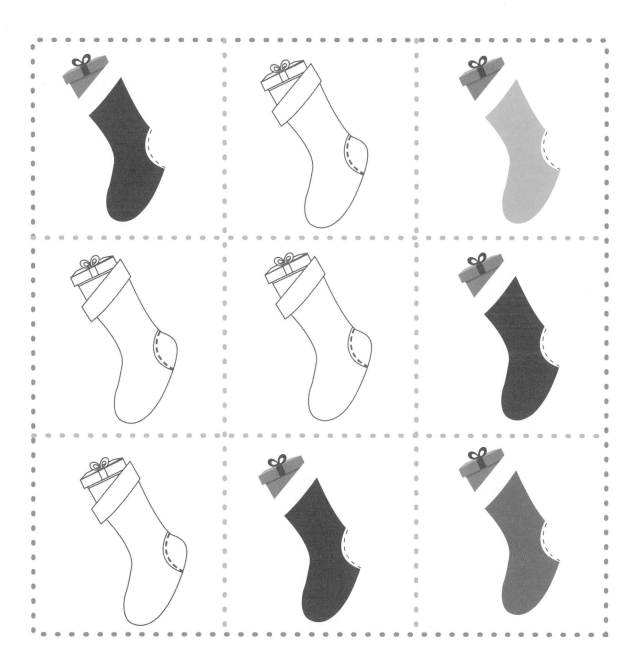

WHERE IS MY SHADOW?

Draw a line from the present to its shadow.

CONNECT
THE DOTS

Connect the dots in numerical order,
then color the picture.

LOGIC

Which Christmas tree should go in the bubble so that each kind of tree appears once in every row and column?

Choose the correct answer.

1   2   3

MATCHING
pairs
The elves have been mixed up.
Draw lines between them to form pairs.

PATTERNS

Look at each pattern carefully
and draw in the missing picture.

196

SPOT THE
DIFFERENCES
Find the 5 differences
between these two sets of mittens.

197

HIDE
and seek
Find these objects in the picture and circle them.

WHAT DOES
NOT BELONG ?
Circle the pieces of clothing
that are not worn in winter.

SUDOKU

Fill in all of the empty boxes so that:
• Each row contains the numbers 1 through 4.
• Each column contains the numbers 1 through 4.
• Each square 2 x 2 box contains the numbers 1 through 4.

 1  2  3  4

WORD
search

Find the hidden words. They may be written horizontally, vertically, or backwards (right to left or bottom to top).

```
I U G L O V E S
G T O O L K I P
L O T G A C T S
O E T S Z A B Q
O B E L L S M B
```

SACK

BELLS

IGLOO

GLOVES

CONNECT THE DOTS

Connect the dots in alphabetical order, then color the picture.

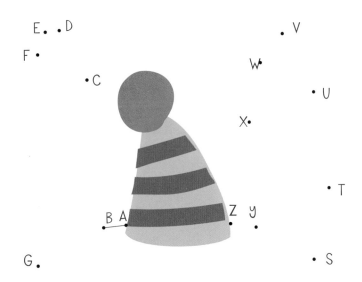

WHERE IS MY SHADOW?

Draw a line from the rabbit to its shadow.

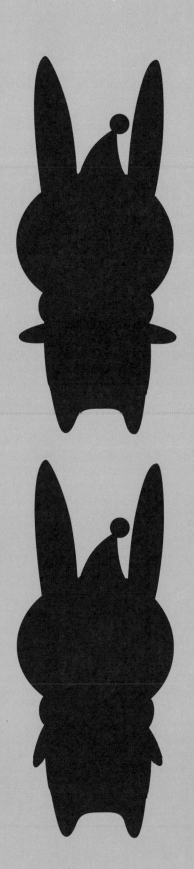

WHAT DOES NOT BELONG?

Can you find this reindeer?

ADDING UP

How many of each owl do you see?
Write your answers in the bubbles.

CODE
maze

Enter the maze and follow
the code to reach the exit.

SPOT THE
DIFFERENCES
Find the 7 differences
between these two pictures.

MAZE
Help the snowman find the present.

210

COLORING
MaGiC

Use the color code to color the wreath.

WHERE IS MY SHADOW?

Circle the penguin's shadow!

ADDING UP

How many Christmas trees can you count on this page?
Write your answer in the bubble.

DRAW A
SNOWMAN
Learn how to draw a snowman,
then draw a few on this page.

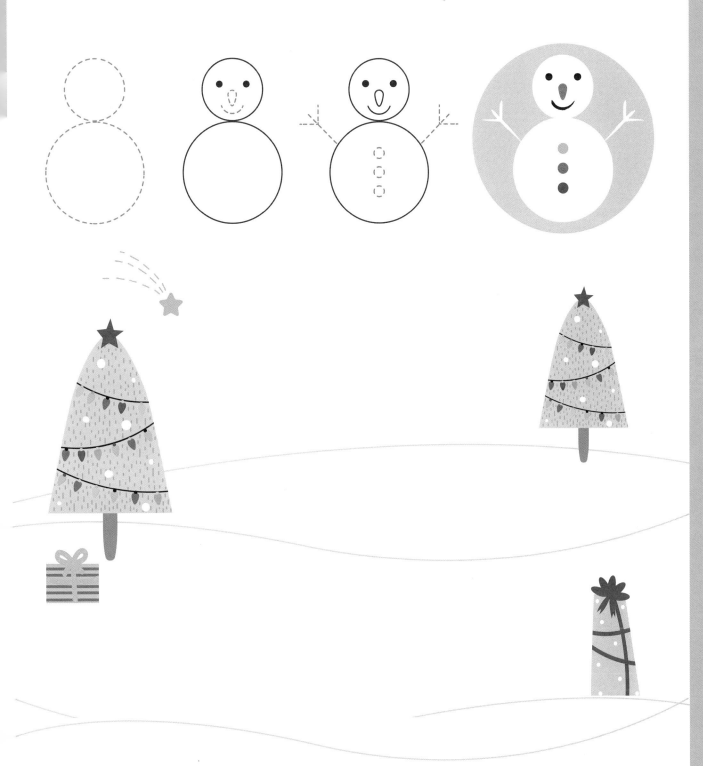

HIDE
and seek
Find these objects in the picture,
then circle them.

DRAW A
WINTER HAT

Learn how to draw a winter hat,
then draw one on each child's head.

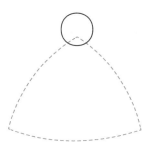

MAZE
Help Santa Claus find the reindeer.

WHAT DOES NOT BELONG?

One of these sweaters is not like the others.
Find the sweater that does not belong.

ADDING UP

How many pine trees do you see in this pretty picture?
Write your answer in the bubble.

CODED
message
Use the code to unscramble the message.

A   E   I   O   U

CHR STM S

 V

DRAWING
Decorate the tree with pretty ornaments and lights.

THE RIGHT PATH

Which path should Santa Claus follow to get to the reindeer?

ADDING UP

How many owls can you count on this Christmas tree?
Write your answer in the bubble.

WHERE IS
MY SHADOW
Cirlce the house's shadow!

227

CODE
maze

Enter the maze and follow
the code to reach the exit.

Enter

Exit

SUDOKU

Fill in all of the empty boxes so that:
- Each row contains the letters A, B, C, and D.
- Each column contains the letters A, B, C, and D.
- Each square 2 x 2 box contains the letters A, B, C, and D.

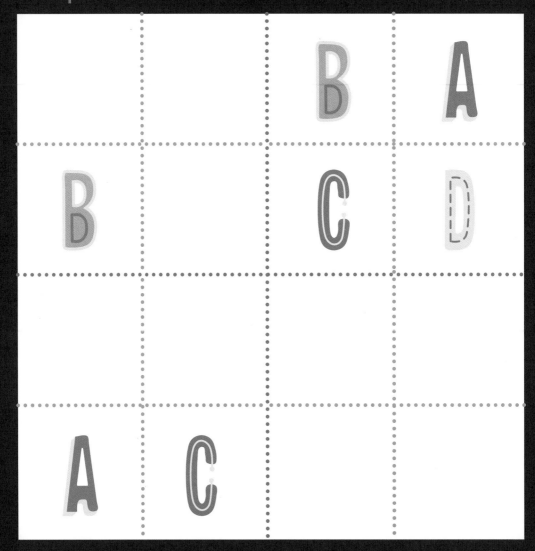

WHAT DOES NOT BELONG?

Can you find this Christmas tree?

231

ADDING UP

How many mittens can you count in this drawing?
Write your answer in the bubble.

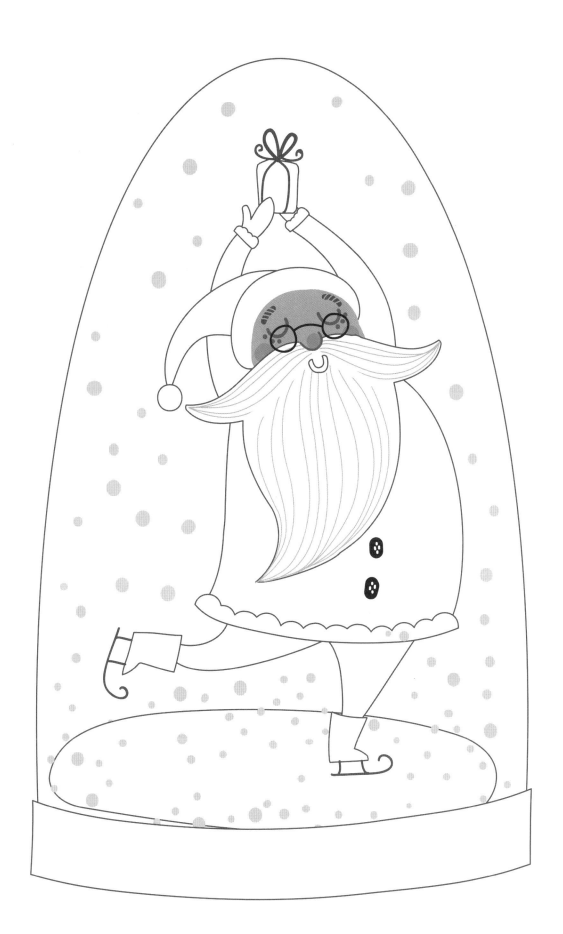

CODED
MESSAGE
Use the code to unscramble the message.

A   E   I   O   U'

 M RRY CHR STM S

 ND

 H PPY N W Y R!

CONNECT
THE DOTS

Connect the dots in numerical order,
then color the picture.

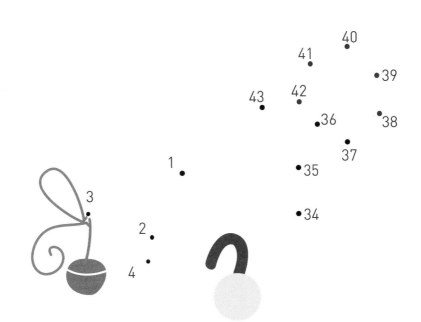

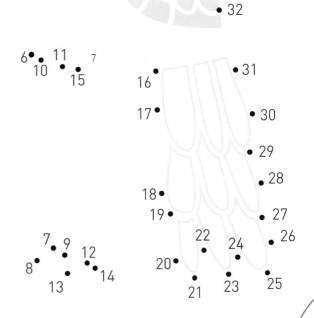

STOCKING Pairs

One of these stockings is not part of a matching pair.
Can you find it?

DRAW
a PENGUIN

Learn how to draw a penguin,
then draw a few on this page.

WHAT DOES NOT BELONG?
Can you find this penguin?

WORD
search

Find the hidden words. They may be written horizontally or vertically or backwards (right to left or bottom to top).

winter

coal

TOY

TUNECOAL
ONVWUTIN
YHLOERPV
EWINTERQ
TLYSEQEB

SNOW

240

WHAT DOES NOT
BELONG IN THE SLED?
There are 4 objects in this picture that
do not belong. Can you see them?

DRAW A
CHRISTMAS TREE
Learn how to draw a Christmas tree, then draw a few on this page.

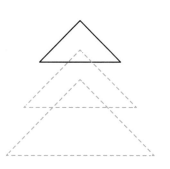
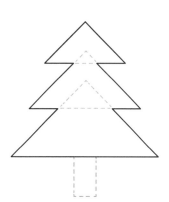

COOKIE
Pairs
One of these cookies does not have a partner. Find which one it is!

MAZE

Help Santa Claus find the gingerbread man.

SPOT THE
DIFFERENCES
Find the 4 differences between these two pictures,
then color in the drawing below.

ADDING UP

Count the objects below and write
how many you find of each one in the bubbles.

MERRY CHRISTMAS!

SOLUTIONS

P. 29 :

P. 35 :

P. 51 :

P. 61 :

3	1	2	4
2	4	3	1
4	2	1	3
1	3	4	2

P. 65 :

Logic: Answer 1

P. 73 :

P. 79 :

P. 85 :

C	D	B	A
B	A	D	C
A	B	C	D
D	C	A	B

P. 95 :
Ornaments: 6-5-7

P. 101 :

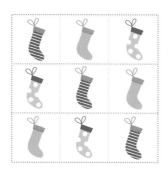

P. 111 :

P. 121 :

P. 127 :
7 presents,
6 ornaments

P. 133 :

P. 138 :

250

SOLUTIONS

P. 139 :

P. 140 :

P. 141 :

P. 142 :

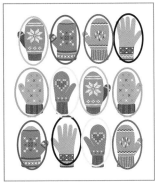

P. 144 :
4 foxes

P. 145 :

P. 146 :

P. 147 :

P. 148 :

P. 150 :

P. 151 :

P. 152 :

P. 154 :

P. 156 :
At Santa's workshop.

SOLUTIONS

P. 157 :

P. 158 :

P. 159 :

P. 160 :

P. 161 :
Logic: Answer 2

P. 162 :

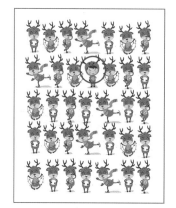

P. 164 :
The elves are making toys.

P. 165 :

P. 168 :

P. 172 :

P. 174 :
9 stockings, 7 reindeer

P. 176 :

P. 178 :
Logic: Answer 2

P. 180 :

P. 182 :
I can't wait to open my presents.

P. 184 :
9 winter hats with a pompom

P. 186 :

SOLUTIONS

P. 188 :
Logic: Answer 2

P. 190 :

P. 191 :

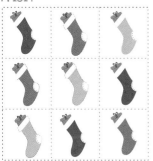

P. 192 :

P. 193 :

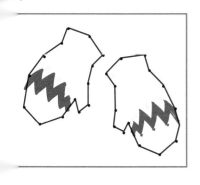

P. 194 :
Logic: Answer 3

P. 195 :

P. 196 :

P. 197 :

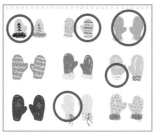

P. 198 :

P. 200 :

P. 201 :

3	4	2	1
2	1	4	3
1	2	3	4
4	3	1	2

P. 202 :

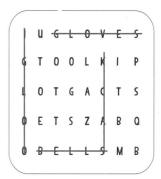

P. 204 :

253

SOLUTIONS

P. 203 :

P. 205 :

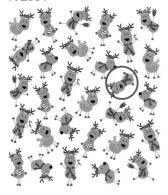

P. 206 :

P. 208 :

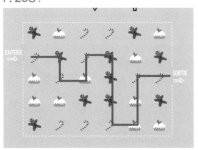

P. 209 :

P. 210 :

P. 212 :

P. 214 :
12 Christmas trees

P. 216 :

P. 218 :

P. 220 :

P. 221 :
11 pine trees

P. 222 :
Christmas Eve

P. 224 :

P. 225 :
26 owls

P. 226 :

SOLUTIONS

P. 228 :

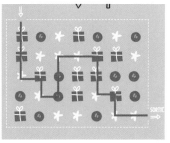

P. 236 :

P. 244 :

P. 230 :

P. 238 :

P. 246 :

P. 231 :

P. 240 :

P. 247 :

P. 232 :

mittens

P. 242 :

P. 248 :

P. 234 :

Merry Christmas and Happy New Year

P. 235:

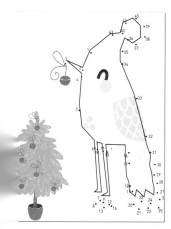